Young Architects 20
Objective

T0278288

Young Architects 20
Objective

Acknowledgments by
Rosalie Genevro
Foreword by
Claire Weisz
Introduction by
Anne Rieselbach

Anya Sirota
Akoaki

Bryony Roberts
Bryony Roberts Studio

**Gabriel Cuéllar
and Athar Mufreh**
Cadaster

Coryn Kempster
Julia Jamrozik
and Coryn Kempster

Dan Spiegel
SAW // Spiegel
Aihara Workshop

**Lap Chi Kwong
and Alison Von Glinow**
Kwong Von Glinow

The Architectural
League of New York

Published by
The Architectural League of New York
594 Broadway, Suite 607
New York, NY 10012
www.archleague.org

ANDREA MONFRIED EDITIONS
www.andreamonfried.com

Distributed by ORO Editions
www.oroeditions.com

To read interviews with each firm,
please visit archleague.org.

Editor Anne Rieselbach
Managing Editor Catarina Flaksman
Cover Design Pentagram / Jena Sher
Interior Layout Jena Sher Graphic Design

This publication is supported, in part,
by public funds from the New York
City Department of Cultural Affairs in
partnership with the City Council
and the New York State Council on the
Arts with the support of Governor
Andrew M. Cuomo and the New York
State Legislature.

The 2018 League Prize program was
also made possible by Elise Jaffe + Jeffrey
Brown, Hunter Douglas Architectural,
and Tischler und Sohn.

Installation photos at Parsons
School of Design at The New School
© David Sundberg/Esto

Library of Congress Control Number:
2020931341
ISBN 978-1-7321608-1-1

Contents

Acknowledgments
Rosalie Genevro
Executive Director, The Architectural League of New York

It is reassuring that even in our chaotic and confusing world, architectural work of high quality—architecture that brings to consciousness the interaction between social organization and space, seeks to create a better public realm, and creates beauty—continues to be produced by successive cohorts of young designers. The League Prize for Young Architects + Designers succeeds, year after year, in eliciting and spotlighting work by exceptionally talented individuals and firms from around North America.

The success of the program springs from many sources. Each year a new committee of past winners brings fresh perspectives and benefits from the expertise of League program director Anne Rieselbach. Each year, Anne and League program manager Catarina Flaksman run the multipart program—competition, exhibition, digital programming, lectures, book—with deep enthusiasm for the individuals and the work. We thank 2018 Young Architects + Designers Committee members Neeraj Bhatia, Molly Hunker, and William O'Brien Jr. for shaping the competition, as well as Tatiana Bilbao, Jorge Otero-Pailos, Georgeen Theodore, and Claire Weisz, jurors invited by the committee. Michael Bierut and Britt Cobb of Pentagram designed, once again, a powerful graphic identity for the theme created by the committee.

Christiane Paul, Kristina Kaufman, Daisy Wong, Daniel Chou, and the School of Constructed Environments at Parsons School of Design at The New School are indispensable collaborators in presenting the exhibition and lectures. Photographer David Sundberg/Esto generously documents the exhibition every year. This book has benefitted from the painstaking attention of managing editor Catarina Flaksman, graphic designer Jena Sher, and advisory editor and friend of the League Andrea Monfried. This book is a copublication of The Architectural League and Andrea Monfried Editions.

Finally, thank you to our financial supporters: the Next Generation and J. Clawson Mills Funds of The Architectural League; Elise Jaffe + Jeffrey Brown; Hunter Douglas Architectural; and Tischler und Sohn. The League Prize is also supported, in part, by public funds from the New York City Department of Cultural Affairs in partnership with the City Council and the New York State Council on the Arts with the support of Governor Andrew M. Cuomo and the New York State Legislature.

Foreword
Claire Weisz
Juror, founding partner, WXY Studio

"Before it even begins": this is a phrase that encapsulates the significance of the League Prize. In her first words to the audience at one of the lectures by the six League Prize winners, Anya Sirota noted that she liked to be called a young architect. The phase of being perceived as "just starting"—and therefore open to opportunity—is a period critical in the evolution of an architect's personal and professional life. The chance encounters and collaborations, the planned debate and dialogue, lead to both a deeper understanding of self and a heightened comfort with risk-taking.

The League Prize puts forward a specific theme as a lens through which to present a series of projects; ultimately, it is a self-assessment by an architect or designer of his or her design process and social contribution. Objective, the topic selected by 2018 committee members Neeraj Bhatia, Molly Hunker, and William O'Brien Jr., evaluated whether the architectural portfolio allows young designers to translate the inherent meaning of objectivity. In addition to the submissions, the winners' lectures and the group exhibition provide different perspectives on the objectivity or subjectivity of site and cultural conditions.

The 2018 Prize winners, as a group, propose that the architect takes on a new role: activating the built environment. This mission goes beyond the performative aspects of architectural and spatial design, particularly sought after in recent years, by incorporating the idea that the structure supporting these aspects should be evocative, dynamic, or literally able to bend or move. The works presented by the winners make a strong case for performance as both architecture understood and architecture experienced. Take Sirota's work: she designs settings for activism and engagement, settings that cannot be understood until they are used and reused for a performance, meeting, or other public action. If a performance is conceived, designed, and planned, just as a building or landscape is, why are they considered different things?

Performance as both experience and critique, as proposed in Bryony Roberts's work, suggests that collaboration is a technique through which to incorporate multiple subjectivities. In the collaborative projects *We Know How to Order* and

Marching On, she uses grids and paving patterns to transmit the important and hidden history of marching bands in a racist and segregated America. As Roberts notes, the marching band should be understood as "a form of camouflage [that allows] the performers and the planners to create an ephemeral experience of political and social realities of public space." Such events make it possible to hold out hope for the significance of architecture and performance in the "post-truth" era.

The concept of objectivity inspired numerous other connotations and reactions. By identifying the need to appeal to a broad audience and offer multiple uses, architects have created a reason to look outside current trends in materials and design inspiration. The concept of "all," referencing an inclusive audience for architectural discourse, is a way of asserting objectivity. Lap Chi Kwong and Alison Von Glinow discuss familiar or domestic forms as a means to connect people from a variety of backgrounds. The reinterpretation of a familiar type—model home, tabletop, crown molding—can lower barriers of understanding, pushing against the isolation of architecture as taught and practiced today.

Many of the League Prize winners shared techniques and methodologies they created to allow a personal perspective—the intuitive, the unwritten—to influence the trajectory and purpose of their projects. Coryn Kempster applies the procedures of oral history to fill a void in architectural knowledge: objective records and subjective memories provided by those who lived and worked in famous modern buildings. The outlook gained from these inquiries pervades other projects, such as *Full Circle*, which uses a circle of swings to promote dialogue that is as physical as it is verbal. Says one user, "It's so much more than a swing set to us."

Gabriel Cuéllar and Athar Mufreh of Cadaster claim that young architects question "to what extent the environment, our profession, and our work are predetermined and predesigned by the system." One answer asserts that architecture is the "network of relations that move the matter around us." Their study of rural churches revealed a network of historic freedman churches that link African American communities across Fort Bend County and highlight the complex issues, including land politics, that face the remaining churches as urban sprawl spreads.

It is no accident that I end this foreword going backward. When my partner, Mark Yoes, and I received the League Prize in 1993, it was both a different time and the same time. In the early years of our work together, we too occupied the space, objective and subjective, provided by the League. The presence of Rosalind

Krauss on the jury inspired us to apply despite our lack of a practice or shared built work. Her call to action—"No longer do we accept the 'sublimation model' according to which 'the function of art is to sublimate or transform experience, raising it from ordinary to extraordinary, from commonplace to unique, from low to high'"— seemed just as critical to us then as it does now in relation to the current crisis of subjectivity.

It seems apt to conclude with the idea that architecture has the capacity to respond to a deep need for connection. By sharing not only his own personal history but that of his mother and even Robert Venturi's mother, Dan Spiegel shows that his built work is an embodiment of architecture as inherited and passed on, that the portfolio still stands as a translator of information, verbal and nonverbal, ideological, spatial, and emotional. In thinking about the future of design and its effect on the ways and means of individual "practices," it is evident that moving forward requires moving backward—there is no one direction. The League Prize winners' eloquent acknowledgment of this state of affairs is one factor that will improve and enhance the world of design.

Introduction
Anne Rieselbach
Program Director, The Architectural League of New York

Objective, the 2018 theme for the Architectural League Prize for Young Architects + Designers, explored the concept of objectivity in architecture, defined by the Prize committee as a set of values that motivates architects to "go beyond personal preferences, and in doing so create a value set of 'truths'—from aesthetics to program to function." Entrants were asked to address objectivity as simultaneously esteemed and undermined in an era in which technology, science, and post-truths coexist and to consider "how objectives and objectivity inform and create values in their work."

League Prize winners presented their work in lectures and as part of the annual exhibition at the Sheila C. Johnson Design Center at Parsons School of Design at The New School. Despite the programmatic and formal diversity of the projects and practices, this year's winners used conceptually related approaches—stylization, distillation, and repetition of key design elements—to convey the underlying design strategies that shape their work.

Five freestanding models arrayed diagonally across the gallery illustrated the work of Akoaki, a partnership between Anya Sirota and artist Jean Louis Farges that fuses design, social enterprise, and planning for cultural events. The models layered water-jet-cut steel silhouettes in saturated powder-coated colors to articulate elements of each project's site and structure. Among the projects were a mobile DJ booth in the form of a space module, a nomadic clip-on gilded archway, and a portable opera set. The models, juxtaposed against backdrops of vacant warehouses, open landscapes, and industrial sites, "suggest ways architectural objects can activate urban scenarios through cultural programming," says Sirota. Graphic and pop, the mockups, much like the studio's full-scale interventions, "explore ways architecture can engage broad audiences and participate in public discourse."

Bryony Roberts's exuberant design for vinyl-printed stone, generated by the hexagonal grid of the gallery floor, filled a gallery wall. The installation was an extension of *Marbles*, studies of medieval geometry and stonework Roberts initiated at the American Academy in Rome. Inspired by the intricate patterns of semiprecious stone in floors in Rome, these studies explored "how the texture of a material can complicate and subvert a geometric pattern." On V-shaped shelves aligned with the printed stone tiles were portfolios and videos of projects by Bryony Roberts Studio, including *Inverting Neutra* at the Neutra VDL Studio and Residences, Los Angeles; the performance *We Know How to Order* at the Chicago Architecture Biennial; and Roberts's collaboration with Mabel O. Wilson, *Marching On*, a performance at Marcus Garvey Park and exhibition at Storefront for Art and Architecture.

Cadaster's installation documented the firm's approach to analyzing urban patterns and their own planning initiatives, focusing on the elements that principals Gabriel Cuéllar and Athar Mufreh identify as "comprising the architecture of territories: parcels, rights-of-way, and watersheds." Contextual analyses and mapped design proposals outlined some of their "territorial interventions," including Subversive Real Estate, a project exploring the historic landholding patterns of Black churches in Houston; Preemptive Watershed, an urban plan for the Twin Creeks area of Kansas City; and Headwater Lot, an adaptive reuse proposal that repurposes the street network of Quebec City. The combination of drawings and supplemental material illustrated forms of land division, a topic that both initiates and informs Cadaster's work. Spanning the length of the installation was a video that projected itineraries through the office's project sites.

An overscaled triangular yellow-green rack held postcards featuring work by Coryn Kempster's firm, Julia Jamrozik and Coryn Kempster. The collection of images was organized into three categories—social infrastructures, expanded preservation, and domestic narratives. Among the projects documented were *Full Circle*, a circular swing set constructed on a vacant lot in Buffalo; *Growing up Modern*, an oral history project based on the recollections of children who grew up in important early modernist dwellings; and Sky House, a residence in Stoney Lake, Ontario. Intended to reflect the firm's aesthetic sensibility and broader design agenda, the rack and postcards provided a "colorful, familiar, unprecious, and accessible framework that invited interaction," said Kempster. He described the cards as "analog prompts in a digital age." Visitors were encouraged to take their favorites in the hope that the postcards would "spark small moments of exchange and conversation when they leave the gallery."

Dan Spiegel presented nine models of projects designed by SAW // Spiegel Aihara Workshop, his partnership with landscape architect Megumi Aihara. Square, uniformly sized, and set into poplar shadow boxes, the white-basswood models were, Spiegel noted, "cut in unconventional ways in order to isolate particular 'loaded moments.'" Natural and artificial light, including LED lighting within the models, modulated the perception of each project. Works on display included Low/Rise House in Menlo Park and a competition entry for Harvey Milk Plaza in San Francisco. Spiegel described the linear arrangement of the models as "intentionally abstract and ambiguous in scale, but also specific in the expression of detail." The installation related to a concept Spiegel explored in his competition portfolio: objects are often defined by the viewer's perception at a single moment in time.

Kwong Von Glinow depicted *Table Top Apartments*, a project for housing that revisits the typical single-story inhabitation of common domestic space. The open framework of the large, linear plywood model appropriated the structural elements of a table: the tabletop as roof or ceiling, the legs as supporting columns. Basic geometric forms—circle, square, and rectangle—generated three types of plans. The resulting combinations, according to partners Lap Chi Kwong and Alison Von Glinow, "create a diversity of spatial experiences," and the interstitial spaces generated by four stories of living spaces form "vertical courtyards, providing dense, diverse, open, and light-filled spaces for residents to enjoy together." Kwong and Von Glinow describe these courtyards as "functional collisions" that "allow for the limitless potential" of shared space.

The League Prize call for entries suggested that an objective "implies an action" and that "how we act, what our actions achieve, and how we argue for a design speak to our values as a discipline and as a society." The work of the winners exemplified the wide-ranging ways in which young architects and designers are pursuing multiple "objectives," from projects that address social, economic, and political agendas to material and structural experimentation that inspires innovative and meaningful design at every scale.

Biographies

Anya Sirota / Akoaki
Detroit, Michigan

Akoaki is a Detroit-based architecture and urbanism studio founded in 2008 by Anya Sirota and Jean Louis Farges. The practice explores ways in which culture and context can prompt novel, inclusive, attractive environments. By emphasizing networks, interdisciplinary design processes, and programming strategies, Akoaki has established a reputation for innovative and resonant projects that engage the social, spatial, and material realities of place.

Akoaki has received an ACSA Faculty Design Award, a SXSW Eco Place by Design Award, and an R+D Award from *Architect* Magazine. The studio's recent work has been exhibited at the Saint-Étienne International Design Biennale, Vitra Design Museum, Chicago Cultural Center, ADAM–Brussels Design Museum, and Detroit Institute of Arts.

Sirota received a BA in modern culture and media from Brown University and an MArch from the Harvard University Graduate School of Design, where she was awarded the Araldo A. Cossutta Prize for Design Excellence. She is an associate professor and associate dean at the University of Michigan Taubman College of Architecture and Urban Planning. Sirota also directs the ArcPrep program at the University of Michigan Research Studio in Detroit.

Bryony Roberts / Bryony Roberts Studio
New York, New York

Bryony Roberts Studio is a design and research practice based in New York City. Founded in 2011 by Bryony Roberts, the office approaches design as a social practice, creating immersive environments and community-based collaborations that respond to complex cultural histories. Combining tools from architecture, art, and preservation, the studio has created transformative design projects in Rome, Dubai, New York, and Los Angeles and has exhibited at the 2015 Chicago Architecture Biennial and at Performa 17.

Roberts received a BA from Yale University and an MArch from the Princeton School of Architecture, where she was awarded the Suzanne Kolarik Underwood Prize. Since founding her own practice, she has received the 2015–16 Rome Prize from the American Academy in Rome, a summer 2018 MacDowell Colony fellowship, and the 2018–19 J. Irwin and Xenia S. Miller Prize. Roberts has published her research in *Harvard Design Magazine, Log, Future Anterior,* and *Architectural Record*; co-edited the volume *Log 31: New Ancients*; edited *Tabula Plena: Forms of Urban Preservation*; and is editing the forthcoming *Log 48: Expanding Modes of Practice*. She teaches architecture and preservation at the Columbia University Graduate School of Architecture, Planning and Preservation in New York.

Gabriel Cuéllar and Athar Mufreh / Cadaster
Minneapolis, Minnesota

Cadaster is an architecture practice founded in 2016 by Gabriel Cuéllar and Athar Mufreh. The office explores the relationship between architecture and urban conditions through research and design projects. Cadaster believes that architecture exists objectively because of its connections—physical, legal, political, social, economic, ecological, conceptual, geographical, historical—to a surrounding context. The practice takes on this mess, triggering, tuning, and transposing the web of relations that gives meaning to space and physical constructions. The goal rests more in taking a position regarding context and defining a role for architecture than in idiosyncratic making.

Cuéllar received a BArch from Carnegie Mellon University and an MArch from the Berlage Institute (Netherlands). He was the 2018–19 Oberdick Fellow at the University of Michigan. Mufreh received a BArch from Birzeit University (Palestine) and a masters in integrated urbanism and sustainable design from Stuttgart University and Ain Shams University (Cairo). Mufreh and Cuéllar currently teach at the University of Minnesota.

Coryn Kempster / Julia Jamrozik and Coryn Kempster
Buffalo, New York

Julia Jamrozik and Coryn Kempster endeavor to create spaces, objects, and situations that interrupt the ordinary in engaging and playful ways. Their multidisciplinary practice operates at a variety of scales and durations, from temporary installations to permanent public artworks and architectural projects. Their academic research focuses on the role of play in the built environment and on alternative methods of documentation as a form of historic preservation.

Kempster received a BA from the University of Toronto and an MArch from the Massachusetts Institute of Technology. Before moving to Buffalo to pursue his practice with Jamrozik in 2015, he worked at Herzog & de Meuron and at Harry Gugger Studio, both in Basel, Switzerland. He is an adjunct assistant professor in the department of architecture at the University at Buffalo SUNY.

Current projects include the book *Growing up Modern*, an interpretive farm education center for kids, and public artworks in Cleveland, Ohio, and Lethbridge, Alberta. Jamrozik and Kempster have received three grants from the Ralph C. Wilson, Jr. Foundation and KaBoom! for permanent play sculptures in disadvantaged communities in western New York and have been invited to represent Buffalo at the 2019 Seoul Biennale of Architecture and Urbanism.

Dan Spiegel / SAW // Spiegel Aihara Workshop
San Francisco, California

Dan Spiegel founded San Francisco–based SAW // Spiegel Aihara Workshop with his partner, landscape architect Megumi Aihara, in 2014. Their work makes use of the productive tension between architecture and landscape architecture. Instead of delving into the oppositions that typically arise when landscape and architecture are considered separate disciplines—interior/exterior, synthetic/natural, contained/continuous, or formal/informal—SAW is concerned primarily with conceptions of experience over time.

Spiegel received a BA in public policy from Stanford University and an MArch from the Harvard University Graduate School of Design. He teaches architecture at UC Berkeley College of Environmental Design. SAW has received an AIA Emerging Professionals distinction and has been recognized as one of *Architect* Magazine's "Next Progressives" and *Architectural Record*'s "Design Vanguard."

Lap Chi Kwong and Alison Von Glinow / Kwong Von Glinow
Chicago, Illinois

Kwong Von Glinow is a Chicago-based architecture practice founded by Lap Chi Kwong and Alison Von Glinow in 2017. Their investigations center around urban public space, city living solutions, and spaces for cultural engagement, translating architectural concepts into playful designs for a broad audience. The office takes an explicitly optimistic approach to design, evident in the motto "Enjoy Architecture."

Kwong received a BA from the University of Washington and an MArch from the Harvard University Graduate School of Design. He has worked at Herzog & de Meuron in Basel, Switzerland, and Amateur Architecture Studio in Hangzhou, China. Kwong is an adjunct professor of architecture at the Illinois Institute of Technology.

Von Glinow received a BA from Barnard College and an MArch from the Harvard University Graduate School of Design. She has worked at Herzog & de Meuron, SOM, Toshiko Mori Architect, and Svendborg Architects. Von Glinow was a 2017–18 Forefront Fellow with the Urban Design Forum in New York. Kwong and Von Glinow received a 2019 Graham Foundation grant for their project *Smuggling Architecture*.

Anya Sirota

Akoaki

We make objects with big ambitions for application in complex urban scenarios. Legible, blingy, and culturally calibrated, our objects-cum-scenographic-constructs explore architecture as an instigator of social transformation and novel urban morphologies. Departing from the instrumentalized benevolence of architecture's newly rediscovered social conscience, we combine aesthetic and political concerns agnostically. Each effort is both experimental and proactive: we seek out potential sites, formulate catalytic programs, convene diverse publics, and secure external funding before embarking on a design. In this way, we hope to address a longstanding criticism of architecture—that it relies on and services constituencies of power.

Treating our constructs as means rather than ends, we pursue a practice that resituates architecture in the realm of planning and equitable development. This paradoxical objective is driven by multiple desires: first, to transcend the constraints of economic austerity and enlist more diverse constituents; second, to treat architecture as a medium to create more ambitious, equitable, and emancipated possibilities; and third, to design spaces capable of popping the algorithmic social bubbles that keep groups of people apart. The studio is committed to generating alluring environments even with the implicit challenges of our approach.

Materializing these aspirations, however partially, requires a shrewd attitude. We are convinced that furtive institutional infiltration is more efficient at instigating change than dogmatic, boots-on-the-ground resistance. Against a contemporary backdrop of volatility, tribalism, and social unrest, we firmly believe that creating space for animated encounter, assembly, and provocation is one way to change perception and move forward.

The Mothership
Detroit, Michigan, 2014

At the height of Detroit's blight-remediation campaigns, which preceded the city's 2013 bankruptcy, the prospect of a tabula rasa urbanism seemed imminent. Thousands of homes, abandoned or foreclosed, were razed in the city's economically challenged neighborhoods, making way for a projected recovery.

In response to the municipal bulldozing, we launched *The Mothership*. A nomadic DJ booth/conceptual space vehicle/urban marker, the capsule explored ways to calibrate practice and apply iconicity in order to give form to the underexposed cultural narratives of place. In Detroit's North End, *The Mothership* channeled the Afrofuturist sensibilities of George Clinton's Parliament-Funkadelic stage prop of the same name, referencing the vanguard funk, soul, and R&B venues that once animated the neighborhood's main thoroughfare. The module moved between open lots and vacant buildings as it broadcast experimental, locally rooted cultural programming and instigated irrepressible revelry.

Glossy, gold, and multichrome, the capsule's cosmetic finish borrowed techniques from car customization. Billowing smoke added to the illusion of a space landing. Despite the strategic showiness, however, the unit was assembled by means of bolts and a simple paneling system. Packed flat, it was easily transported in the back of a pickup truck.

opposite, top:
Vinyl-and-dichroic-film-embellished aluminum panels

opposite, bottom:
The Mothership stationed at the ONE Mile garage

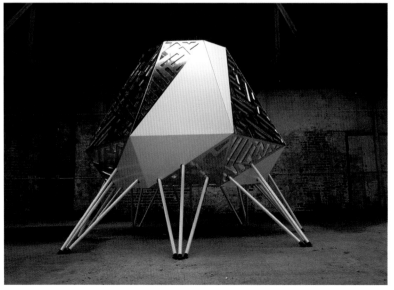

top: DJ Jami Tata

bottom: *The Mothership*
activating a vacant lot
Photo: Kirk Donaldson

below:

Construction diagram

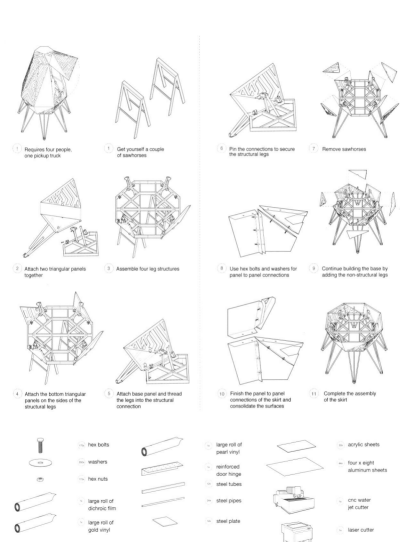

1. Requires four people, one pickup truck

1. Get yourself a couple of sawhorses

6. Pin the connections to secure the structural legs

7. Remove sawhorses

2. Attach two triangular panels together

3. Assemble four leg structures

8. Use hex bolts and washers for panel to panel connections

9. Continue building the base by adding the non-structural legs

4. Attach the bottom triangular panels on the sides of the structural legs

5. Attach base panel and thread the legs into the structural connection

10. Finish the panel to panel connections of the skirt and consolidate the surfaces

11. Complete the assembly of the skirt

17a hex bolts

36b washers

17b hex nuts

1a large roll of dichroic film

1a large roll of gold vinyl

1a large roll of pearl vinyl

1a reinforced door hinge

12b steel tubes

24a steel pipes

12a steel plate

30a acrylic sheets

4a four x eight aluminum sheets

1a cnc water jet cutter

1a laser cutter

Pop Stars
Amilly, France, 2013

We constructed two monumental stars, thirty feet from point to point, at a defunct tannery 120 kilometers south of Paris. One star hovered delicately above the exhibition space, clipped to a concrete beam, while the second stepped between columns on the ground floor, balancing precariously over the tannery tanks. The two protagonists functioned as three-dimensional supergraphics in dialogue with the idiosyncrasies of the industrial building as well as with the landscape beyond.

Titled *Pop Stars*, the project examined ways in which architectural installations can advocate for the preservation of post-industrial sites. Floating signifiers visible from multiple vantage points, the stars encouraged visitors to take a fresh look at the spatial potential of an industrial property in an undone state. The construction itself was a performance, with the site open to the public for a month while the installation was designed, prototyped, and assembled, according to the logic of stud construction, using simple tools: mill saw, table saw, pneumatic stapler, and screw gun.

We conceived the project at a critical time: local authorities were contemplating a conventional restoration strategy for the tannery complex. With interior surfaces removed and concrete structure bared, however, the surviving architecture offered liberty for experimentation and interim engagement. *Pop Stars* aimed to reveal the spatial opportunities inherent in deconstructed and unresolved environments.

opposite, top:
Stripped industrial
interior as backdrop

opposite, bottom:
One star balancing over
the tannery tanks

Nomadic Culture Council Arch

Detroit, Michigan, 2016

The Nomadic Culture Council hosted a series of public assemblies convened by artists and cultural leaders seeking to address the need for a department of cultural affairs in Detroit. The events brought together arts advocates, curators, policy makers, educators, philanthropic organizations, and cultural activists to formulate the shape and aspirations of such an entity in the post-bankrupt city.

To accommodate the series of public meetings, we created a marker in the form of a clip-on architectural threshold. The 21-foot *Nomadic Culture Council Arch*, composed of architectural replicas, contemporary art objects, and landscape elements, paid tribute to the enduring allure of Detroit's taste for ornament and embellishment. Simultaneously, it served as a sign that temporarily transformed existing structures into stately, though ephemeral, public institutions. A situational prop, the arch made a case for architectural installation as an instrument of public discourse, materializing a collective aspiration by giving form to an imaginary parallel institution.

opposite: DJ Los
posing with the arch
Photo: Anne Laure Lechat

opposite, top: Saint-Étienne International Design Biennale, 2017
Photo: Anne Laure Lechat

below: Elevation with symbolic components

opposite, bottom: ONE Mile garage

 a. Mothership

 b. Detroit Free Press D

 c. Papyrus camamiform

 d. Reuben Telshkin speakers

 e. Thoth mask, Space is the Place

 f. Pheasant

 g. Bobcat, Power-House Productions

 h. Nagesh sneaker

 i. Packard Plant boats

 j. Sun Ra breast plate

 k. Fisher Theater arch

 l. Egyptian column

Anya Sirota **29**

Detroit Funkestra
Detroit, Michigan, 2016

Detroit Funkestra was designed as deployable scenography for a three-act, open-air opera. The piece, produced in collaboration with the Detroit Afrikan Music Institution, was first performed at the Oakland Avenue Urban Farm in Detroit's North End. Twelve local musicians representing a breadth of genres were positioned among kale and hibiscus plants and recounted an incomplete history of music in the city.

The set, much like the opera itself, was conceived as a playful mashup. Sampling colors, shapes, and material finishes from existing and disappeared performance stages at music venues in the neighborhood, the installation offered a nostalgia-free graphic reconfiguration of historic elements. Calibrated to look both familiar and renewed, the stage served as a subliminal backdrop designed to support activity in a neo-rural scenario.

Using 400 discrete fragments of plywood bolted together on site, *Detroit Funkestra* created an ephemeral cultural infrastructure. More important, the project instigated a social experiment—it introduced performance and theater as mechanisms for a more nuanced understanding of urban space and the embodied actors who give it meaning.

opposite: *Detroit Funkestra* installed at Oakland Avenue Urban Farm

top: Musicians Emily Rogers, Duminie Deporres, Onyx Ashanti, and Zach Land performing in front of the *Detroit Funkestra* stage set
Photo: Doug Coombe

bottom: *Detroit Funkestra* reconfigured for the 2017 Saint-Étienne International Design Biennale
Photo: Anne Laure Lechat

a.

b.

perspective 1

c.

d.

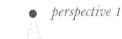

perspective 1

perspective 2

a.

b.

d.

c.

perspective 2

Detroit Cultivator
Detroit, Michigan, 2017

Detroit Cultivator is a multidisciplinary effort to transform the six-acre Oakland Avenue Urban Farm into an experimental urban prototype to counter gentrification and forced displacement in an economically vulnerable neighborhood. The plan blends agriculture, culture, business, and stewardship of the environment in a civic commons that is economically, ecologically, and culturally sustainable.

In addition to uniting productive and leisure landscapes, the project reworks a number of vacant structures for public programming. *The Landing*, a two-family residence, is reconfigured as a hostel and gastronomic performance center; *Little Big Box*, a former grocery store, offers flexible event space with a commercial kitchen and housing; and *Red's Jazz Shoe Shine*, a legendary cobbler shop and speakeasy, is reestablished as an experimental music venue.

Detroit Cultivator positions urban agriculture as a grassroots redevelopment strategy that benefits marginalized neighborhoods by thinking holistically about community needs. Simultaneously, the plan works toward new, diversified, and interdisciplinary methods to support a nascent urban typology.

opposite, top:
Model of six-acre site
Photo: Jacob Lewkow

opposite, bottom:
Detail of *The Landing*
Photo: Jacob Lewkow

top: Section-perspective of *Red's Jazz Shoe Shine*

bottom: Section-perspective of *Little Big Box*

The Beta Movement
In collaboration with Steven Christensen Architecture
WUHO Gallery, Los Angeles, California, 2011

WUHO Gallery, a small storefront venue on Los Angeles's storied Hollywood Boulevard, invited us to participate in its program of architectural exhibitions, which focused on contemporary issues in representation. In view of the glitz and glamour of the context—the Academy Awards, the Walk of Fame, and Hollywood's canonical theaters—the gallery seemed quaint, humble, virtually invisible. Against the force and vitality of the entertainment industry, typical exhibition subjects—the formal preoccupations of architecture—appeared outmoded.

As we confronted the reality of the streetscape and the inscrutability of the exhibition space, we focused on temporary performance sets as a spatial strategy. This concept led us to stage a spatial transformation in lieu of a polite architectural exhibition. Part scenographic intervention, part inhabitable supergraphic, the installation explored direct engagement with multiple publics. We imagined the project as a grand-scale, transitory, self-propagating "selfiematon" that invited tourists and Angelenos inside for their own red-carpet moments.

Stars from the famous sidewalk inspired our own stars, which we projected through the gallery to produce a series of spatial distortions. Replete with filmic references to superheroes, hyperspace, hypnotism, evil lairs, and astrophysical singularities, the space encouraged visitors to act performatively. The rough qualities of the exposed plywood and stud construction revealed the temporary nature of the illusion. Cuts through the plywood slices filling the gallery led to a projection room where a video and text presentation described the formal procedures at play.

opposite, top:
Installation
Photo: Steven Christensen

opposite, bottom:
Plywood, studs, paint

below: Project
diagram and
geometric strategy

**opposite, top
and bottom:**
Installation views
Photos: Steven Christensen

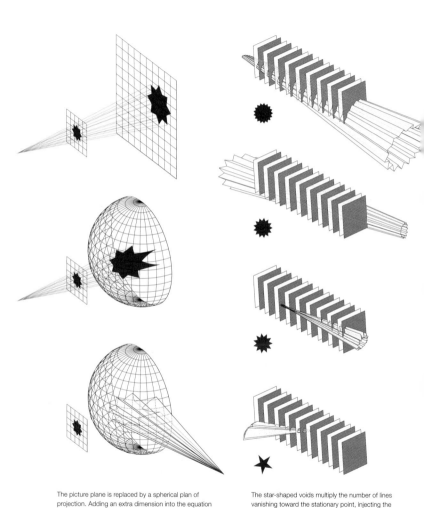

The picture plane is replaced by a spherical plan of
projection. Adding an extra dimension into the equation
yields forms that accelerate and decelerate.

The star-shaped voids multiply the number of lines
vanishing toward the stationary point, injecting the
familiar architectural device of forced perspective
with a healthy dose of steroids.

General Manifold
In collaboration with Steven Christensen Architecture
Chelsea, Michigan, 2012

As part of our investigation into various occupations of post-industrial sites—in this case, public inhabitation of a private property—we lodged an immersive architectural environment into the boiler room of an abandoned 80,000-square-foot Federal Screw Works plant about 60 miles west of Detroit. The installation, a response to the derelict context, provided a moment of surprise and punctuation within a larger choreographed experience for visitors and urban explorers. We carved a mysterious magenta void from the perceived solid of the factory's central space, generating a site of geometric complexity, chromatic contrast, and optical distortion. From the exterior, the space appeared to have been turned inside-out—a poor man's homage to Anish Kapoor's *Leviathan*. On the interior, a series of precise cuts in the truncated pyramids produced an effect of perspective overlay, inviting visitors to question the depth, dimension, and scale of this aberrant environment.

Inside the "unsolicited" pavilion, titled *General Manifold*, visitors encountered a six-channel soundscape consisting of spatially localized and syncopated industrial sounds layered over readings of seminal eighteenth- and nineteenth-century texts about ruins by John Ruskin, Viollet-le-Duc, Bernardin de Saint-Pierre, and Denis Diderot. A playful jab at the ubiquitous proliferation of "ruin porn" imagery in the post-industrial landscape, the sound installation was produced in collaboration with model and former Playboy Radio host Brandie Moses.

opposite, top:
Interior view of pavilion
Photo: Steven Christensen

opposite, bottom:
Pavilion inserted into
factory boiler room
Photo: Steven Christensen

Bryony Roberts

Bryony Roberts Studio

... partial, locatable, critical knowledges sustaining the possibility of webs of connections ...
—Donna Haraway

Bryony Roberts Studio works at the intersection of architecture, preservation, and social practice, examining how social histories shape the architecture of a specific site and how new design can prompt alternative forms of occupation and interaction. At this edge between the tangible and the intangible, objectivity is impossible; instead, the practice seeks the promise of overlapping, partial perspectives. As Donna Haraway writes in "Situated Knowledges," every individual's viewpoint is shaped by the particularities of cultural context and historical moment. Embracing situated knowledges, the studio cultivates the discord of multiple points of view, finding the disconnects and commonalities among an original author, successive authors, contemporary inhabitants, and new design methods.

The studio develops methods of expanded site-specificity, creating design projects in response to existing architecture as well as to layers of social history. Throughout the design process, the studio interviews and works with people inhabiting a site and develops collaborations with local creators. The result is a feedback loop between research and design, and between collective and singular authorship.

Formally and materially, the projects celebrate decorative and performative arts that are often marginalized within contemporary architecture. Textiles, ornament, pattern, performance—all have long cultural histories and can offer accessible, interactive environments for multiple audiences. Bringing playful colors, textures, and events to the large scale of public space, the practice prompts new modes of occupying familiar architectural spaces.

Primo Piano
American Academy in Rome
Rome, Italy, 2016

Primo Piano is an installation that responded to the unique stone floor of the entryway at the American Academy in Rome and referenced the tradition of patterned stone floors throughout the city. The floor in the foyer of the 1914 McKim, Mead & White building displays a modest, neo-Renaissance pattern of travertine circles and diamonds set into peperino stone. Elsewhere in Rome, medieval Cosmati floors present circles, triangles, and squares in more intricate patterns, which indicated the positions of clergy and worshippers during religious celebrations. *Primo Piano* used adhesive vinyl shapes to create a new pattern, producing a visual oscillation between the existing floor at the American Academy and superimposed references to surrounding medieval and baroque precedents. Disrupting the axial, symmetrical organization of the entry, the design introduced alternative directions for movement and attention in the space, which both emerged from and defied the existing geometry.

Project team: Daniel Clark

opposite, top:
Foyer of American
Academy in Rome

opposite, bottom:
Installation view

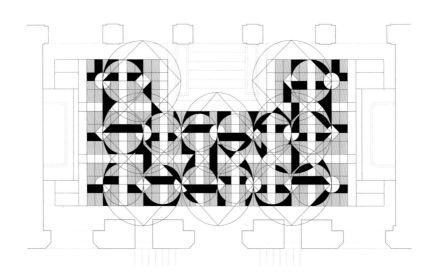

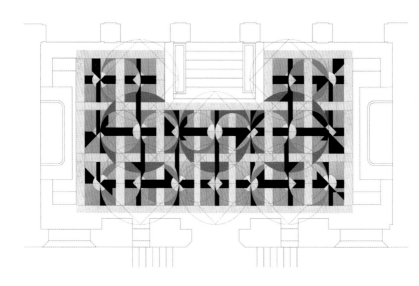

Marching On
In collaboration with Mabel O. Wilson and the Marching Cobras of New York
New York, New York, 2017–18

Marching On is a research project, performance, and exhibition that explores African American marching performances as acts of cultural expression and political resistance. With a history rooted in military training, nineteenth- and twentieth-century African American marching bands both honored service in U.S. conflicts and protested the nationwide lack of civil rights. While the movements, costumes, colors, and iconography of marching performances have expanded dramatically since the nineteenth century, in part due to the influence of hip-hop and step choreography, marching bands and drumlines still remain connected to a historical lineage of marching as political expression.

The project was inaugurated with a series of performances in Marcus Garvey Park in Harlem that referenced the revered Harlem Hellfighters as well as the 1917 Silent March against racial violence. The choreography for these events was developed with the Marching Cobras of New York, a Harlem-based after-school drumline and dance team.

The exhibition combined the research and the performance into a spatial installation. In the past, marching bands often served as a form of camouflage, enabling African Americans to gather in large groups during the era of Jim Crow segregation. Starting from this concept of concealment, the exhibition featured triangular fabric panels printed with camouflage patterns interspersed with historical and contemporary images. The fabric changed color along the length of the gallery, inviting viewers to duck and weave between panels to discover thematic topics related to the history of race and urban public space.

Project team: Sadie Dempsey, Mariam Abd El Azim, Mayra Imtiaz Mahmood

Commissioned by Storefront for Art and Architecture
Supported by National Endowment for the Arts, Graham Foundation, Lower Manhattan Cultural Council, and Performa 17

top: Installation
at Storefront for Art
and Architecture
Photo: Miguel de Guzman,
Imagen Subliminal

bottom: Performance
by the Marching Cobras
in Marcus Garvey Park
as part of Performa 17
Photo: Jenica Heintzelman

opposite, top:
Concept image

opposite, bottom:
Performance by the
Marching Cobras in
Marcus Garvey Park
Photo: Jenica Heintzelman

below: Concept image

We Know How to Order
In collaboration with Asher Waldron and the South
Shore Drill Team
Chicago Architecture Biennial, Chicago, Illinois, 2015

Mies van der Rohe's Federal Center in Chicago is a monument of modern
architecture and a symbol of national government, one that is unified by a
relentless and ever-present grid. The three-building complex was set in motion
by Mayor Richard Daley in the late 1950s, at a time of great investment in
the downtown Loop and comparable disinvestment in the predominantly African
American South Side of Chicago. Responding to both the Federal Center and
its larger social history, *We Know How to Order* was a dynamic performance
by the South Shore Drill Team, a youth organization from the South Side. Merging
military drill routines and hip-hop choreography, the group turned the lines
of the Miesian grid into an electrifying system of movement. The transformation
challenged the current militarization of public space and the longstanding
segregation of urban space in Chicago.

**opposite, top and
bottom:** Performance
Photos: Andrew Bruah

Bryony Roberts **55**

Marbles
American Academy in Rome
Rome, Italy, 2016–17

These studies were inspired by patterned stone floors in Rome, in which semi-precious stones are cut and inlaid into intricate geometric patterns. In particular, the project looked at the medieval Cosmati floors of central Italy, in which simple geometric forms—squares, diamonds, and circles in different marbles—accumulate to form complex fields of texture. The floors demonstrate that complexity can emerge not only from geometric permutations but also from the use of different materials within uncomplicated patterns. The color and veining of different marbles produce surprising continuities, contrasts, and optical illusions between adjacent pieces.

The *Marbles* collages explore permutations of medieval Cosmati geometries and of new patterns that draw from historic precedents. Testing the possibilities of inherited geometries, these studies use new marbles created by digitally superimposing existing stones. As architectural drawings, they experiment with representing space not through line but through the juxtaposition of color and texture.

Untitled
The Architectural League Prize
for Young Architects + Designers Exhibition
New York, New York, 2018

This installation features an exuberant graphic composition of faux-stone patterns that emerges from the hexagonal grid of the gallery floor. The project is an extension of *Marbles*, a study of medieval geometry and stonework initiated at the American Academy in Rome. In addition to the vinyl wall and floor graphics, the installation incorporates a zigzag table that displays portfolios of the studio's past projects. The tabletop consists of mitered birch plywood; it is mounted on welded steel legs that align precisely with the pattern affixed to wall and floor.

Project team: Sadie Dempsey

opposite, top:
Installation view

opposite, bottom:
Elevation

below: Installation view
Photo: Miguel de Guzman,
Imagen Subliminal

Inverting Neutra
Neutra VDL Studio and Residences
Los Angeles, California, 2013

Inverting Neutra, an installation at Richard and Dion Neutra's VDL House II (1932; 1966) in Los Angeles, explores spatial inversion as a strategy for activating historic architecture. The VDL House is known for a close interlocking of interior and exterior spaces; exterior patios penetrate the house from the street up to the roof terrace. The inversion is accomplished by turning these void spaces into colored volumes filled with hanging blue cords that align with the spacing of the stair module. The intervention both celebrates and subverts the existing architecture. The hanging cords move with the wind and in response to touch, registering climate and movement through the house. In addition, the blue cords are cut along the contours of human activity; they drop low in a seating area and lift up above the main stair. The resulting condition turns the structural logic of the house into a constantly shifting field of color.

Rather than critiquing Neutra or his architecture, the project serves to investigate the schism between preservation and architecture practices. Probing the creativity of transforming existing structures, the design process generated a new sensory environment embedded within and responsive to a found condition. Included as part of the project was a discussion on alternative preservation practices.

Project team: George Abraham, Jesse Cabildo, Avidan Fernandez, Andre Gharakhanian, Kristina Johnson, Corey Pope

Supported by Graham Foundation

opposite:
Installation view
Photo: Jaime Kowal

below: First- and
second-floor plan-
perspectives

opposite:
Installation view
Photo: Jaime Kowal

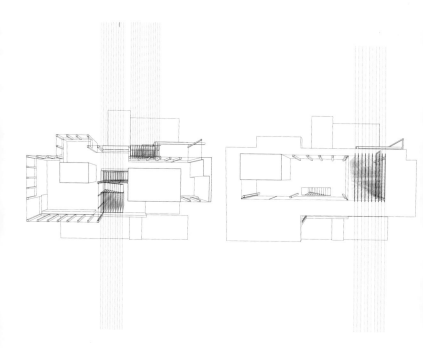

Gabriel Cuéllar and Athar Mufreh

Cadaster

Our work focuses on the architecture of urban conditions. "Urban conditions" does not refer to the scale of a city or region but rather to the forces, institutions, and customs that, in various pervasive and precise ways, shape the surface of the earth. We address questions of how patterns that govern the environment are formed and maintained and how we can help change them or prepare them for change. We consider the practice of architecture as one that extends beyond the specific product of a professional to a network of relations that moves and configures the matter around us. Accordingly, our projects operate on terms broader than a singular site and client, taking on different types of geographies and publics at large.

The forces, institutions, and customs that constitute urban conditions eventually, and often necessarily, take spatial or legal form in the guise of real property, rights of way, jurisdictional boundaries, forms of ownership, property values, zoning ordinances, economic protocols, and remote environmental impacts. Such factors, which have dynamics and characteristics that can be altered, may be used to leverage intervention. Focusing on urban conditions means dealing with these aspects—and their political implications—up front, that is, not accepting them as givens.

In the current landscape of specialization in the design professions, it is difficult to pin down who is responsible for territorial relationships. The result is that key dynamics of the environment are managed by market-oriented entities that operate on the basis of land commodification. For instance, real estate developers have enormous influence in the transformation of the environment, delimiting the field of operations for architects and urban designers. Thus, it is the land development industry, together with a mixed bag of governmental land policies, that today puts forward transformative—and often problematic— visions of urban space and society.

In this milieu, it is important to question the extent to which the environment, and perhaps even architects' work, is predetermined or even predesigned by economic and political structures. If space is first and foremost determined by such factors, what are the ultimate impacts of design interventions?

Subversive Real Estate: The Landholding Patterns of American Black Churches

American South, 2011–18

While the landholding system of the southern United States was devised in part as a means to subjugate Black Americans, the churches of freedmen—former slaves—founded in the late nineteenth century upended the conventions of land ownership. In the decades following the Civil War, landowners and the federal government established a land paradigm based on exclusivity and expropriation. Despite the obstacles in obtaining land within that system, Black churches used real property as a way to build an alternative form of ownership based on collectivity.

This research and activism project emerged from collaboration with the Saint John Missionary Baptist Church of Fort Bend County in Houston, Texas, and demonstrates the degree to which real property registers the extent and nature of power. The terms and geography of land ownership predispose, to a large degree, a region's territorial structure and the ability of its residents to find social and economic stability. The land purchased by Black American churches was typically conveyed under the condition that it would revert to its former owner if it was ever used for purposes other than worship. The churches of freedmen represent a type of landholding that includes rather than excludes, imparting a social value that transcends the potential financial value of a property. Our work explores the ways in which freedmen communities came to obtain land, assert their claims within American society, and establish churches across the South. The freedmen churches serve as a model for generating and sustaining common spaces and, at the same time, shedding light on the workings of real property.

opposite: Map of Fort Bend County, Texas, documenting the more than two dozen freedmen churches

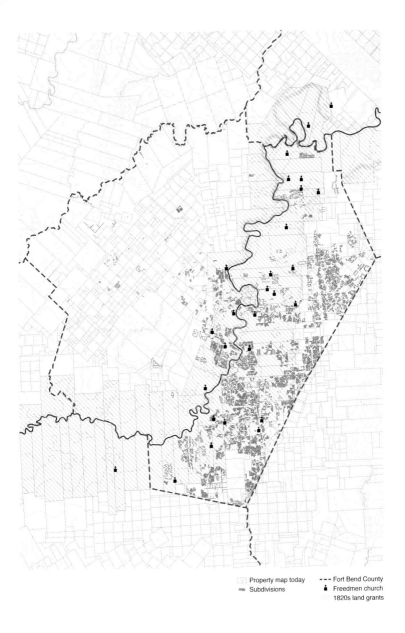

Property map today   --- Fort Bend County
Subdivisions   📍 Freedmen church
1820s land grants

This property is conveyed for church purposes and in event said property ceases to be used for church purposes ... then said property reverts to me or my legal representation.

Mount Olive Missionary Baptist Church, 1907

Any time the house of worship to be built on this land hereby conveyed shall not be used for public worship for a period of six months, then and in that event the title shall revert to the grantor.

Colored Baptist Church of Katy, 1917

The property may only be used for those activities normally associated with a church or open-space/landscape use.

Thompson Chapel Missionary Baptist Church, 1888

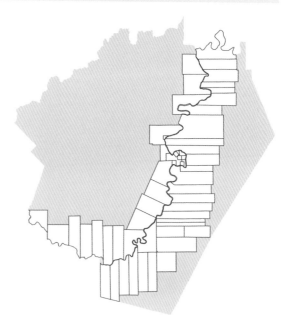

opposite: Colonial land division. In Texas, real property was formed with care. Planters came to hold massive tracts of land and slaves

below: Rural gentrification. Fort Bend County, Houston's expanding suburban frontier, is home to more than twenty-five freedmen churches, all of which face marginalization

Church Circuit: Architectural and Site Rehabilitation of Saint John Missionary Baptist Church of Fort Bend County, Texas

Houston, Texas, 2013–18

In the aftermath of the American Civil War, former plantation slaves, or freedmen, exercised their newly granted right to landownership by building churches across the American South. Despite the widespread discrimination they faced, freedmen built a regional network of rural churches that embodied a radical form of land-holding based on collective use. Today, urban shifts caused by real estate plans threaten these historic sites. Saint John Missionary Baptist Church, one such church, is now embedded in the sprawl of Houston, Texas. This architect-initiated project takes Saint John as the germ of a transformation with the potential to revitalize the freedmen church network and reconfigure the suburban landscape.

The intervention for Saint John facilitates civic engagement with the site by activating its surface. The main features include the preservation of the historic building and construction of a gravel field to host the church's annual homecoming. Throughout the rest of the year, this much-needed open area is available for use by the neighborhood for gatherings and sport. Shifted closer to the street, the church rests on a brick platform that extends to the sidewalk, inviting passersby to visit. A gravel circuit linking these spaces runs along the lot perimeter, offering unencumbered access to the church's extra territory.

opposite, top: Service in Saint John Missionary Baptist Church

opposite, bottom: Church plot surrounded by tract houses, palm trees, swimming pools, and fences

Abandoned 1930s

Church lot
1900–1935

Abandoned 1980s

Colony Lakes
Subdivision

Abandoned 1930s

Church lot 1935–present

Riverstone
Subdivision

Abandoned 2012

Abandoned 2014

Roads
Roads abandoned since 1900
Saint John property line

below: Lumber
framing of church

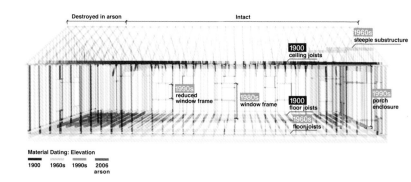

Destroyed in arson — Intact

1960s
steeple substructure

1900
ceiling joists

1990s
reduced
window frame

1980s
window frame

1900
floor joists

1990s
porch
enclosure

1960s
floor joists

Material Dating: Elevation

1900   1960s   1990s   2006
arson

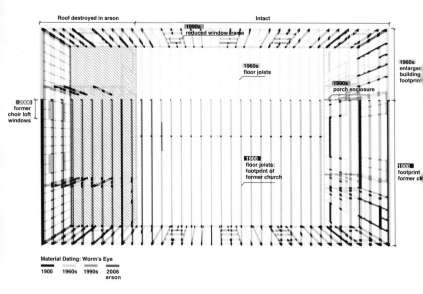

Roof destroyed in arson — Intact

1990s
reduced window frame

1960s
floor joists

1960s
enlarged
building
footprint

2006
former
choir loft
windows

1990s
porch enclosure

1900
floor joists:
footprint of
former church

1900
footprint
former ch

Material Dating: Worm's Eye

1900   1960s   1990s   2006
arson

Preemptive Watershed: Urbanization Plan for Kansas City
Twin Creeks Design Competition Winning Proposal
Kansas City, Missouri, 2016

The Twin Creeks area of Kansas City is a robust natural environment that is nevertheless sensitive to urban development. The current municipal strategy uses a buffer zone that limits development around First and Second Creeks, thereby promoting their ecological balance. However, the creeks offer a crucial recreational, civic, and organizational resource for the city. Thus, the need to conserve the creek corridors is in conflict with the opportunity to put them to use. Our project aims to develop a linear park along the creeks in a way that will shape and guide future patterns of urbanization. The design of the park is thus an ecological task as much as it is an urban design opportunity, drawing on hydrological and built formations on the site as well as on historic and economic conditions.

An invisible network of crests runs across and through the area around First and Second Creeks, establishing a watershed that includes a series of sub-watersheds, or hydrological rooms. The sub-watersheds, though managed individually, share a drainage course and produce the ecological imprint that subdivides the larger Twin Creeks area. Our project uses the sub-watershed as a module for the linear park. Real estate development is managed and the health of the streams is monitored by allowing only incremental growth within these modules.

opposite: Existing territorial imprint of watershed

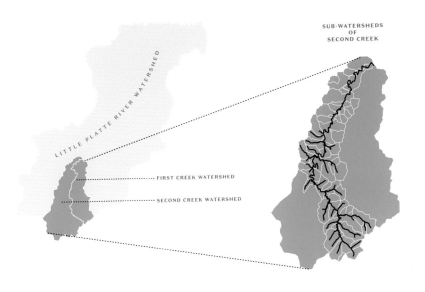

SUB-WATERSHEDS
OF
SECOND CREEK

LITTLE PLATTE RIVER WATERSHED

FIRST CREEK WATERSHED

SECOND CREEK WATERSHED

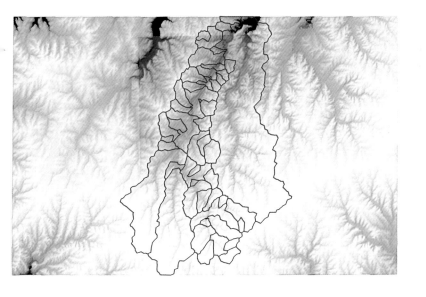

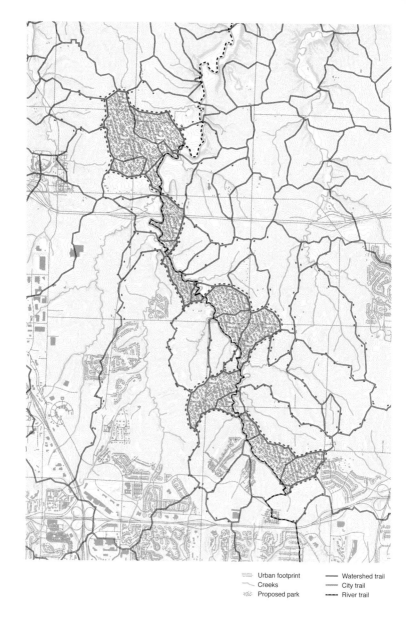

Urban footprint   —— Watershed trail
Creeks   —— City trail
Proposed park   ━━ River trail

opposite: Trail infrastructure for watershed-based urbanization **below:** Three trails following watershed lines. The proposal connects adjacent neighborhoods to the creeks via a trail system

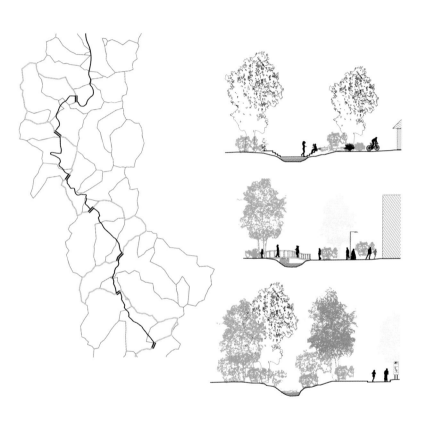

top: City trail

bottom: Watershed trail

top: Riparian trail

bottom: Market park

Headwater Lot: Adaptive Re-Use Plan for the Rights of Way of Quebec City
Reinventing Our Rivers Competition Winning Proposal
Quebec City, Canada, 2017

The St. Lawrence River runs alongside Quebec City and has shaped its identity since the city was founded in 1608. A number of rivers, all tributaries of the St. Lawrence, flow through the city's expansive incorporated area. Each has its own physical characteristics, history, potentials, and challenges, but all share a rich legacy. As part of an effort to safeguard this legacy and establish a new urban program that takes advantage of the waterways, the municipality launched an international call for ideas to rehabilitate Quebec City's major rivers.

We started by looking at seigneurial properties, long narrow parcels resulting from the land distribution system in New France in the seventeenth through nineteenth centuries. Most properties had access to a river, since waterways were essential to livelihood. We proposed re-creating the long lots by repurposing superfluous segments of the road network to develop axes for urban agriculture, bicycle lanes, parks, and storefronts. Each of the Headwater Lots, as we termed them, would lead to a river, thereby reconnecting inland neighborhoods to the waterways. The proposal shows how to apportion and reuse public rights of way, demonstrating that it is possible to adapt urban infrastructure in a way that accommodates different uses and modes of transportation.

opposite: Historic organization of land parcels in Quebec

⬚ Historic towns
— Redundant roads

Headwater lots
— Infiltration streets

top: Headwater Lot with connection to river

bottom: Current development patterns allocate little access to the rivers

Upstate Ecologies: Regional Vision for the New York Canal System
Reimagine the Canals Competition Proposal
New York State, 2017–18

The Erie Canal, which connects New York City to the Great Lakes, was completed in the early nineteenth century, generating new regions of economic and infrastructural development across New York State. Virtually unused today, the canal system left imprints that still structure the multifaceted landscapes and settlements of northern New York. What can the canal infrastructure offer to local communities and visitors? Are there economic synergies that can emerge from the corridor's present conditions? What kind of strategic urban framework would enable a global but nuanced revitalization of the region?

Our project aims to use the urban and ecological diversity along the canal's 360 miles to shape future transformations. More specifically, we identified five frames of reference, or "canal ecologies": rural axis, core, urban outline, satellite, and production corridor. Each ecology encompasses a unique set of conditions that recurs along the canal and typifies sites where settlement, infrastructure, land use, natural landscapes, and economic factors coalesce and interact. We propose both a commercial role and a spatial strategy for each ecology, bringing a regional coherence to the economic and geographic development of the canal system.

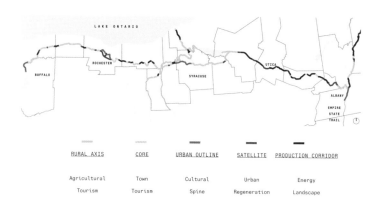

RURAL AXIS	CORE	URBAN OUTLINE	SATELLITE	PRODUCTION CORRIDOR
Agricultural Tourism	Town Tourism	Cultural Spine	Urban Regeneration	Energy Landscape

opposite: Map of the five canal ecologies

right (top to bottom):
Satellite views of canal ecologies: rural axis, core, urban outline, satellite, production corridor

below: Plan and rendering of production corridor, which takes advantage of the vast state-owned lands alongside the canal to develop an energy and logistics landscape

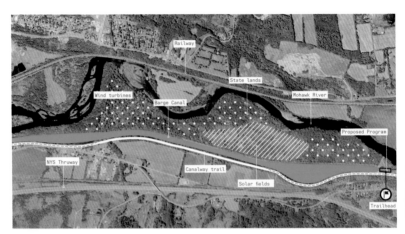

below: Plan and rendering of rural axis, which connects locals and visitors to agricultural producers and heritage sites, producing public spaces that promote opportunities for commerce

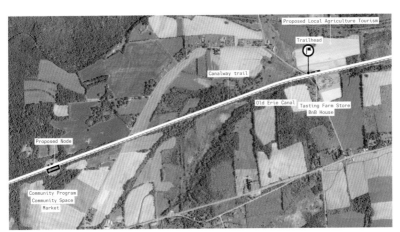

Coryn Kempster

Julia Jamrozik and Coryn Kempster

We find our objectives in subjectivity, in stories told, places visited, and spaces imagined. We find our motivations in conversations with one another and with others. We measure the success of our projects by the memories they create.

Approaching our projects with an open-ended process and few preconceptions, we learn from each context (social, historical, cultural, and physical) with the intent of proposing ideas that are specific, critical, and playful. Working in a range of media and at different scales allows us to explore the themes that interest us (such as social interaction, play, and alternative narratives) through myriad methodologies and forms of expression. Our work can be classified into three interdependent categories: social infrastructures, expanded preservation, and domestic narratives.

Social infrastructures engage individuals in public space by means of playful shared experiences. Analog prompts in a digital age, these structures offer moments of interpersonal connection. In a time of grave disunity in the United States, simple sparks of interaction have the potential to, however briefly, bring people of different backgrounds together.

Expanded preservation questions traditional methods of conservation and proposes modes of representation and documentation that work toward augmenting the factual through individual experience. These projects typically consist of narratives, visual recordings, or installations and offer an alternative to established modes of objectcentric preservation.

Domestic narratives tell stories through everyday spaces by expressing the desires of others and shaping our own projections. By designing spaces from the perspective of a child or imagining scenarios for changing use, we embed idiosyncratic moments into domestic architecture.

Full Circle
Buffalo, New York, 2016

Full Circle stems from an interest in spaces of play as places that can be used to liberate the individual from the generic and to enrich the everyday. The project takes a prototypical playground component, the swing set, and questions its conventional linear arrangement to achieve an abstract, spatial, political, and interactive transformation.

The installation literally twists the typical experience of parallel movement on swings to provide opportunities for confrontation and dialogue. By shaping a piece of playground equipment into a charged spatial arrangement characteristic of political roundtables and corporate boardrooms, we position a playful construct in the adult world.

A vigorous grassroots campaign encouraged teachers, parents, administrators, city council members, community activists, and neighbors to take active ownership of *Full Circle*. As a result, the installation has become known within the neighborhood as a meeting place for children and adults alike. In a community with few maintained green spaces and little public infrastructure, it is a small but significant gesture.

Commissioned by CEPA Gallery and C.S.1 Curatorial Projects

opposite, top and bottom: Installation views
Photo (bottom): Brendan Bannon

Coryn Kempster **101**

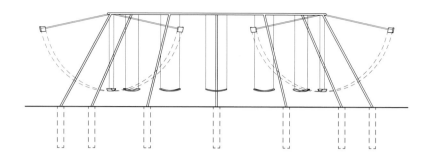

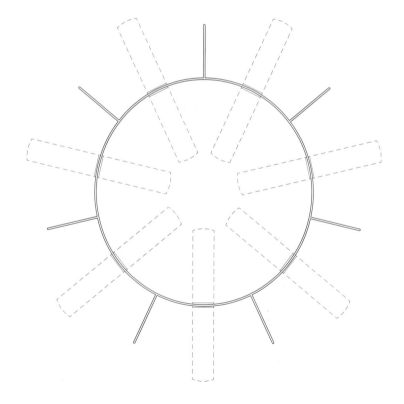

opposite: Elevation
and plan

below: Film still from
See It Through Buffalo,
Paget Films and

University at Buffalo
School of Architecture
and Planning

Vertical Line Garden
International Garden Festival, Jardins de Métis
Grand-Métis, Quebec, 2017

Placed on the grounds of a historic garden, this installation uses contemporary ready-made means and hyper-unnatural materials along with pattern, order, color, and density in a play on traditional formal gardens. Barricade tape, typically employed to delineate a perimeter and keep people out, is here used to bring visitors in and entice them to inhabit the garden.

Vertical Line Garden is a fluid space that responds to environmental conditions, changing dramatically with the intensity of light and wind. Depending on the weather, the space can be kinetic and open or calm and closed but permeable. The transformation is auditory as well as visual: sound generated by the movement of the barrier tape ranges from a quiet stir to a vigorous rustle.

With its canopy of colorful lines, the installation is both graphic and playful. It encourages interaction yet is not prescriptive about use. While adults enjoy the comfort of the custom lounge chairs and take pleasure in moments of repose, youngsters run, frolic, and explore.

Vertical Line Garden is one of nine versions of a project commissioned by Jardins de Métis. *Line Garden* was the first, selected in an open competition in 2014, and *Roof Line Garden*, for the Musée de la Civilisation in Quebec City in 2020, will be the most recent.

**opposite, top
and bottom:**
Installation views

Dialogue
Eastman Reading Garden, Cleveland Public Library
Cleveland, Ohio, 2017

In a time of political and social disunity, we hoped this project would spark discussions outside the boundaries of individual comfort zones. A circle of interlaced sound tubes stimulates conversations that range in length and seriousness, encouraging communication and spontaneous interaction among friends and strangers. While the sound cones are connected to one another, their pairing is not immediately apparent, resulting in a game of questioning and movement as one interlocutor tries to discern the location of his or her counterpart.

Dialogue calls attention to the potential of public space as a place where people from different backgrounds and with different worldviews can interact. At the same time, it highlights the solitary experiences that individuals often create for themselves in the contemporary city: preoccupied users of technology and portable devices, even when surrounded by others, may interact only with the echo chamber of a chosen social media platform. *Dialogue* is thus an analog social infrastructure that cultivates serendipitous connections between people to interrupt and expand their experience of public space.

Commissioned by LAND studio for the annual *See Also* program

below and following
pages: Installation views
Photo (below): Bob Perkoski

Take me with you
The Architectural League Prize
for Young Architects + Designers Exhibition
New York, New York, 2018

For the 2018 Architectural League Prize exhibition we chose to display photographs of our work as postcards on a freestanding bent-metal armature. In the spirit of our built projects and our broader design agenda, the rack and the cards were colorful, familiar, and intentionally unprecious. The three faces of the rack corresponded to the three themes we use to classify our work: social infrastructures, expanded preservation, and domestic narratives.

Overall the display provided an accessible framework that invited interaction. Visitors picked up the cards for a closer look and, as invited by the installation title, helped themselves to those they were most drawn to. We hoped the postcards, as physical prompts, might spark small moments of exchange and conversation not only in the exhibition but also, and more important, afterward beyond the gallery doors.

opposite:
Installation view

Growing up Modern
2015–present

While a lot has been recorded about the clients who willfully dared to pursue modernity in their domestic environments, little is known about the experiences of the children who grew up in some of history's most revolutionary early modernist houses and housing. This research project aspires to document the personal narratives of the serendipitous inhabitants of architectural masterworks in order to bring their memories to a broader audience.

We conducted a series of interviews with individuals who were the first young inhabitants of radical modern buildings of the early twentieth century. We also photographed the buildings, looking for specific views to illustrate the stories we had heard.

Growing up Modern is a foray into oral history, an approach not always available or sought out by architecture scholars. The study questions which histories, and whose histories, are being preserved in relation to these structures. We assert that the recollections of those who have occupied the residences, rich in anecdotal and personal detail, are as worthy of understanding and preservation as the buildings themselves.

opposite, top: Views of Hans Scharoun's Schminke House in Löbau, Germany, with recollections by Helga Zumpfe

opposite, bottom: View of the rooftop at Le Corbusier's Unité d'Habitation in Marseille with recollections by Gisèle Moreau

Even though her family left the dwelling over seventy years ago, Helga Zumpfe (née Schminke) still dreams about the house she grew up in.

The colored glass portholes on the door frames were set at the children's eye level. Helga Zumpfe recalls running from door to door with delight to look at the world through different colors.

Gisèle Moreau heard of Le Corbusier's death on the radio while sunbathing on the concrete rock on the roof terrace. She remembers feeling so close to the buidling, and by extension to its architect, that she thought the news was about her in some way.

In the afternoon, Ernst Tugendhat would play in the sandbox on the upper terrace, listening for the sound of a car horn, which signaled his father's arrival home.

opposite: View of
Villa Tugendhat in Brno,
Czech Republic
by Mies van der Rohe
with recollections
by Ernst Tugendhat
(pictured below)

right and below:
Rolf Fassbaender
holding his childhood
photo album and
view of the row house
by J.J.P. Oud at the
Weißenhofsiedlung
in Stuttgart with
recollections
by Fassbaender

Rolf Fassbaender recalls, "I have great memories of my childhood here. We had a concrete bench, a sunny garden, and in the summer life was outside."

Sky House
Stoney Lake, Ontario, 2017

We received the commission for Sky House just as we were concluding the interviews for *Growing up Modern*. Those conversations led us to appreciate the role that domestic spaces can play in childhood memories and the subtle ways in which small details can resonate even decades later. As a result, we decided to emphasize the wishes and opinions of the clients' daughter, along with those of her parents, in the design process.

Thinking of the many experiences she would have in the holiday home and how these would help define her memories of summer and of her childhood, we designed idiosyncratic moments with the daughter in mind. The approach to the lake house, for example, became an opportunity to signify arrival through a specific visual, auditory, and kinesthetic experience: a sky-blue ramp connects the ground to the main entrance. The wooden boards emulate the experience of a dock and reverberate with the pressure of running feet. In the entry, we placed a checkerboard grid of round pink coat hooks at various heights and sizes to accommodate the child as she grows. In the living room, we designed a fireplace socle of blue glazed bricks where she might snuggle with the family dog. In her bedroom, thinking of sleepovers and the sharing of the space with her friends, we specified a bed as wide as the room. Outside, underneath the bridging volume of the house, we hung a bespoke perforated metal loveseat, creating a place with a view of the lake to escape to with a friend or a book. All of these moments are specific, and while our young client may use these spaces in entirely different ways than we intended, we hope that they will actively or passively become ingrained in the memories she develops in this place.

Sky House was thus rooted in a desire to accommodate personal domestic narratives as much as it was driven by a careful understanding of the site and associated massing, programmatic, environmental, and material strategies.

top: Sky House nestled into the landscape. The lower volume is barely visible upon approach
Photo: Doublespace Photography

bottom: Section-perspective showing overlap of lower and upper volumes and covered outdoor space with loveseat swing

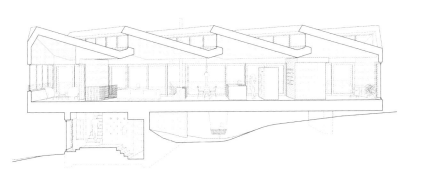

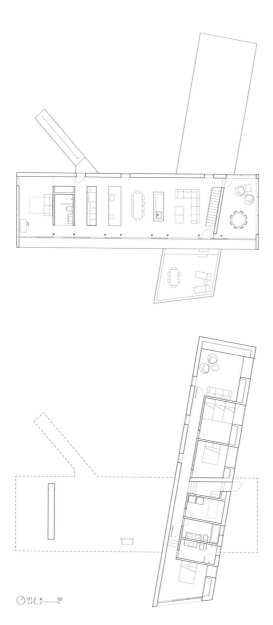

below: Plans of upper and lower volumes

opposite: Loveseat swing under upper volume with path to lake

Photo: Doublespace Photography

below: Upper volume with eighty-foot-long wall of glass facing the lake
Photo: Doublespace Photography

opposite: Tall ceilings and whitewashed plywood walls amplify the daylight in the upper volume
Photo: Doublespace Photography

Dan Spiegel

SAW // Spiegel Aihara Workshop

When I was in architecture school, I went to see a movie about an indie rock band, which somehow turned out to be the story of a singer looking into his late father's work in quantum physics. At some point in the movie there was a cat in a box and then light particles fired at two slits. From what I gathered, it seems there are infinite possibilities for any situation until you observe it. Take a look— and define the object.

There are probably obvious times to observe certain things—the start, the end, maybe the middle. But there are also times you don't expect—after the end, before the beginning. I designed a house around a tree that doesn't exist yet. When the house is built, I'll plant the tree. The tree will grow; but at any given moment, it won't yet be done, but it also won't be incomplete. Choose how you look at a particular time—and set the objective.

My dad is a physician—a psychiatrist, to be specific, not a physicist. His parents were psychiatrists too. They raised him in Long Island, in a house designed by Alfred Levitt. My dad remembers the house as bright, warm, and airy—it stuck with him. The house remained for some time, but Alfred and his family were more interested in the economics of mass-produced housing (namely, Levittown).

This kind of housing seemed like a pretty good idea, but when I went to Florida in 2008, I saw it again, or at least some version of it. All the repetition felt so generic, like isolation or loneliness. At that time, these developments often ended in foreclosure. I heard on the radio that real estate companies would sometimes hire fake families to come in and stage the homes so that they could be sold.

My mom moved around a lot; she never knew who built her family's houses. As a kid she gravitated toward pools of light pouring over the breakfast table— she still does. She talks often about those fleeting conditions of light. I might be reading too much into it, but I think the lesson was: Things change. Kids get older. Families grow and shrink again. So I set out to design an adaptable house . . .

Low/Rise House
Menlo Park, California, 2013

...one that is part tower, part ranch, part horizon. It is supposed to feel like spaces suspended within the landscape, like light particles scattering through slits.

Google Maps discovered this house right after the foundations were poured, which made it seem like that was all the house was for years. Eventually Google came around and observed the site once again. Maybe that's when the house became real.

I've seen the photographs of the house enough times now that it's easy to imagine that their setting is a day, July 27, 2013, rather than a place, Menlo Park. Even so, at certain moments some things seemed taller than usual. Some longer. Some less defined at the edges. Some more continuous. And some entirely fleeting, despite the solid materials. Some things change faster than others.

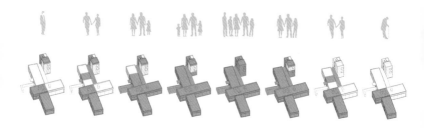

above: A more adaptable house

below: The house
on July 27, 2013

Photos: Bruce Damonte

below: Additional
photographs from
July 27, 2013
Photos: Bruce Damonte

top: Scattered particle plan

bottom: Screengrab from Google Earth several years after construction

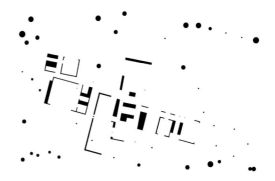

Try-On Truck

California, Colorado, New York, Texas..., 2016

I started to wonder: how do you know what something actually is if it changes every time you look at it? We designed this little structure to change, but in different places, it changes in different ways. On Treasure Island, it changes according to a regular routine: arrive, open the door, fold open the walls, hang the bench and desk, invite people in. Places like Union Square in San Francisco seem to agitate it in other ways. Maybe all the attention requires a bit more privacy, more modesty. Or maybe a bit less? It's meant to be flexible, but this version—a nomadic lingerie store, of course—has changing rooms, algorithms for finding bras, and as much modesty as you're in the mood for.

If I'm being honest, the truck was born from studies of thousands of mobile homes. All are basically the same at the start but pretty different by the end. Someone in Vancouver looked at the unfolded truck and thought of a meditation studio, so he asked us to turn it into one. It's just like the lingerie store, but with more clothes, fewer partitions, more privacy from the outside, less privacy from the inside, and the need to double in size as soon as the truck stops. At least twenty other people from around the world called us with their own sincere, fairly serious ideas of what the truck could be. Eventually, we had to make a chart to keep the projects straight.

Project Team: Dustin Stephens, Mobile Office Architects

below: Some
mobile projects

Coffee Shop
Copenhagen, DK

Christian Bookstore
Mansfield, OH

Women's Clothing Store
Santa Barbara, CA

Cabin
Big Sur, CA

Lingerie Shop
San Francisco, CA

Men's Shirt Tailor
Milan, IT

Guest Apartment
Brooklyn, NY

Skin Care Shop
Los Angeles, CA

Artist Studio
Guerneville, CA

Real Estate Office
Chicago, IL

Sunglasses Shop
Turin, IT

DJ Booth
Palo Alto, CA

Coffee Shop
Copenhagen, DK

Jewelry Shop
Miami, FL

Meditation Studio
San Francisco, CA

Sunglasses Shop
Portland, OR

Casper Labs
San Francisco, California, 2017

I was walking through SoMa and saw a mattress company testing out naps on a truck. Always up for an adventure, I went in. I thought the nap was pretty good, and so I bought a mattress. A few weeks later the company called to ask us to design a new office and workshop. I wish it always happened that way.

They were primarily concerned about where to put the walls to separate the different things they would have to do in rooms. It was a fair point, but we were more interested in the continuity and texture of the ceiling, since we were trying to drape curtains made of steel and hang a cloud made of pillowcases. (Not every client has 117 extra pillowcases sitting in a warehouse.)

So we compromised. There are rooms but not many doors. The walls are solid (usually) but look like fabric. Corners are rare, and walking feels continuous. It's pretty practical when you think about how mattresses and things like that get made. The furniture had to follow the same rules—be solid but act like fabric, avoid corners when possible, and try to maintain some continuity.

Our photographer Bruce saw it that way too on August 25, 2017, though he was mostly standing still.

opposite, top: Entry
Photo: Bruce Damonte

opposite, bottom:
Project rooms
Photo: Bruce Damonte

below: Production plan

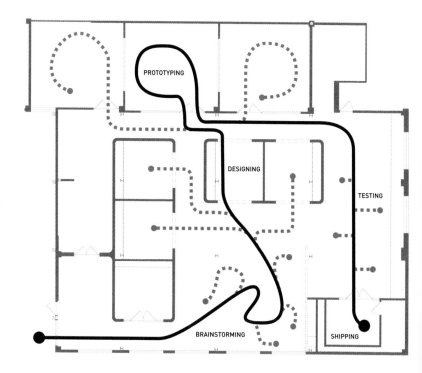

PROTOTYPING

DESIGNING

TESTING

BRAINSTORMING

SHIPPING

Cheyenne River Sioux Tribe Powwow Pavilion

Eagle Butte, South Dakota, 2012–ongoing

A few years ago, Dustin and I spoke with a Sioux tribe from South Dakota. They had been promised some money to build housing. And while money is temporary, traditions last a long time. So we started by designing a pavilion for the annual powwow, which the tribe could build with local materials like rammed earth and straw, keeping investment circulating within the community. Really, we were trying to design a process.

But a process can be a place too, and it can be helpful to have a place to make plans. Each fall, the pavilion gets a little bigger, and the younger generations practice building. Over time, there's more space for the community to gather, practice, plan, and make housing. As the tradition grows, the money stays local. The first of these clusters of structures is still there too, like a physical memory.

Project Team: Dustin Stephens, Mobile Office Architects

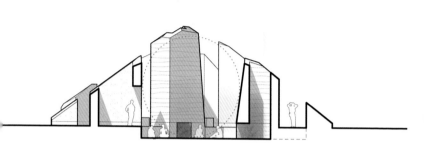

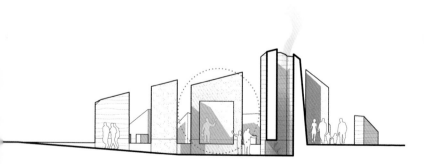

below: Plan, year 3

1. Large Gathering Space
2. Medium Gathering Space
3. Small Gathering Space
4. Low Gathering Space
5. Stage Space
6. Fire Stack
7. Ramp Down

0' 5' 10' 20'

Lockwood BnBnB
Truckee, California, 2016–ongoing

I think it matters when you see a place. If you happen to be in Tahoe on Labor Day, for instance, first you notice the mountains, of course. Then you might see the estates around you and think that they're going to good use. But it turns out that they're empty most of the time. There's a 65 percent residential vacancy rate in the area. Most vacationers come in the summer—something that seasonal workers must find frustrating in the winter when they struggle to find housing amid the empty rooms. Sometimes you need a whole house, but often you need just part of one. And everyone has different ideas about when to visit, so why not work with that? Maybe everyone would benefit from sharing.

Consider MLK weekend. On January 20 (for instance), the homeowner and her family wake up in the red tower; friends from Vermont play with their kids in the green tower; and three lift operators from Chile, here for the season, rent space in the blue tower. Over breakfast, the youngest lift operator tells the couple from Vermont about the best trails, while Grandma walks in from the red tower and reads stories in front of the fire to the children she just met.

You can divide up the towers, but you don't really need to. And if you ever run out of room, you can always add a tower and connect it. Most of the action is in the spaces in between, which look a little different every day.

top: Perspective
of some interactions

bottom: Section,
mostly of your space

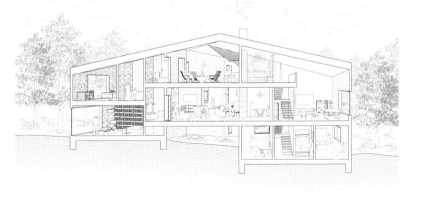

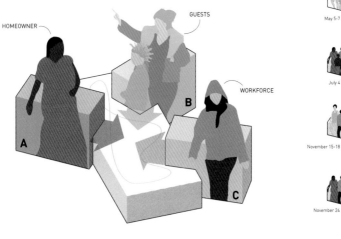

HOMEOWNER

GUESTS

WORKFORCE

A

B

C

May 5-7

July 4

November 15-18

November 24

December 10-11

opposite, top:
Perspective,
spaces in between

opposite, bottom:
Co-living scenario,
January 20, 2020

below (bottom to top):
Plans for one, two,
and three families

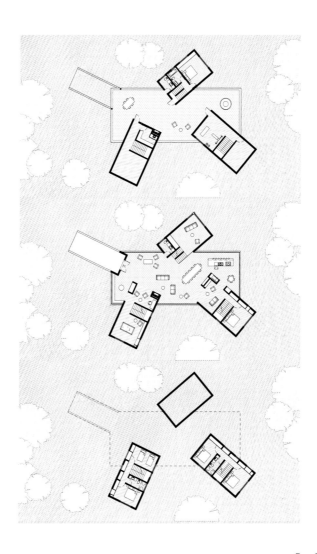

A-to-Z House

San Francisco, California, 2016

Several years ago I met a San Francisco couple with the most unusual house: low and free-standing and seemingly overwhelmed by the city. It really was a totally typical house—but for a different place. They asked me to design an extension to the house—up and over for the views, and a bit bigger and more connected. I kept drawing the elevations as carefully as I could, but I have to admit that I didn't realize the western light would turn half the windows gold, and the eastern light would turn the other half blue. The building was pretty accurate, but the trees grew during construction, and the shadow patterns were hard to anticipate. The couple got pregnant and had twins by the time the house was done. It's hard to see, but in those drawings, the house had lots of space. In the photos, you can tell there is just barely enough.

opposite, top:
East facade
Photo: Bruce Damonte

opposite, bottom:
East elevation

below: Stair between levels
(barely enough space);
plans, first and second
floors (enough space)
Photo: Bruce Damonte

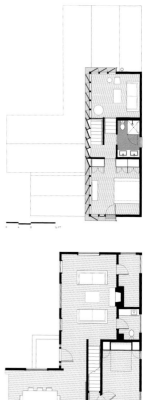

Lap Chi Kwong and Alison Von Glinow

Kwong Von Glinow

We design with two methods: *smuggling architecture* and *borrowing the familiar*.

Act 1: *Smuggling Architecture: House XYZ, Crowns,* Ardmore House

smuggling architecture
verb
1. to conceal an architectural agenda
2. to inject architectural significance into topics that have disappeared from the discipline of architecture

The pairing of *smuggling* and *architecture* is purposeful. *Smuggling* presupposes that what is being smuggled is small, or at least small enough to be hidden. *Architecture*, however, is big, bold, and built. *Smuggling architecture* actively works with this juxtaposition: seeking to conceal an architectural agenda while knowingly exposing itself to interaction as built space.

   Smuggling architecture injects architectural significance into topics that have lost their connection with the discipline. We see this design strategy as the beginning of a series of interventions that engage with a larger audience to foster an interest in architectural values where architecture has previously not been present.

Act 2: *Borrowing the Familiar: Grand Lattices, Table Top Apartments, Towers within a Tower*

The pairing of *borrowing* and *familiar* is how we relate our design process back to the user, the culture, and the territory. *Borrowing* is our way of neighborly reusing. The *familiar* speaks to the collective, to memory, to a common understanding. It has a legibility and specificity. The familiar is relatable—we get it. The familiar takes away the need for acquaintance: we are already familiar. The familiar is form: primitive figures, primary geometries. We make architecture by *borrowing the familiar*.

   Borrowing the familiar stems from the belief that architecture should connect to the people who use it. We see this design strategy as a tangible means to make architecture accessible to a broad public. Ultimately, we borrow to share.

House XYZ

2017

What does it mean to live in a house where any space can be used in any direction? What happens when there are no obstructions—corridors, multiple floors, even interior walls? Can the suspension of the dimensional create a new way of thinking about life in a house?

When people imagine being in their houses, they might begin by navigating through it conventionally. Without much thought, residents can close their eyes and envision how to reach each area, or what they can do in each area. They think about these things without considering any thresholds or efforts they would need to pass through or exert to get from point A to point B. The sequence of movements can be shuffled: occupants can skip right from the downstairs kitchen to the upstairs laundry room. *House XYZ* provides a setting for this type of movement. It brings together everything that makes a house a place of domesticity—a bed for sleeping, a tub for bathing, and a kitchen countertop for cooking—without the physical constraints of walls and floors. Domestic items are suspended from ceiling cables; a cable track in the ceiling inscribes the circulation that occurs three-dimensionally. "Rooms" are configured by means of X, Y, and Z coordinates, creating an invisible plan in which all spaces are visually and physically accessible.

below: Domestic items
placed according to
X, Y, and Z coordinates

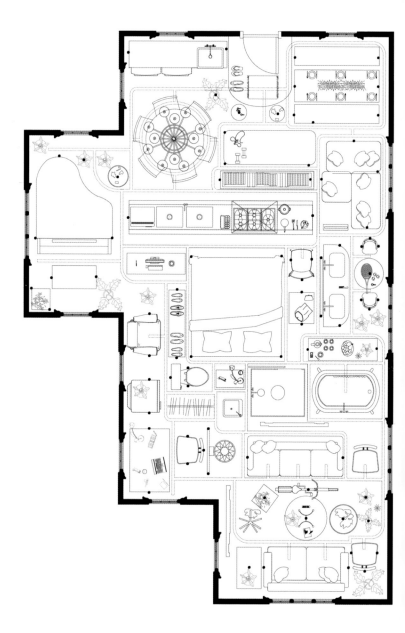

opposite: Plan resembling a storage warehouse

below (clockwise from top left): Bathing, eating, playing music, lounging

Crowns
Volume Gallery
Chicago, Illinois, 2018

Crowns was an architecture installation at Volume Gallery in Chicago. It included a series of crown molding artifacts liberated from the context of a suburban house. Four of these overscaled constructs occupied the large space and retraced the familiar profiles of crown molding.

The significance of crown molding in the everyday house is twofold: first, it presents itself as part of a domestic aesthetic; second, it acts as an eraser that builders can use to cover up unnegotiated details. It is because of these characteristics that crown molding has been ignored by modernism. In this installation, crown molding no longer acts cosmetically, camouflaging a joint, but rather exists independently, tracing seams to become the object itself.

opposite, top:
Model

opposite, bottom:
Crown objects

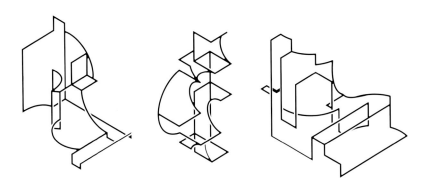

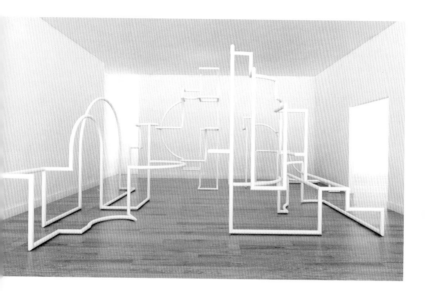

Ardmore House
Chicago, Illinois, 2019

Single-family homes typically take on a client's needs and aesthetic requirements to make tailor-made houses. Architecture then becomes limited to fine details and expensive material exploration, with perhaps some minimal room for spatial experimentation. While such a process is a valid design route, we decided to use the conventions of the single-family house to investigate how this generation and the next are living and will live.

What we found is that Millennials—and perhaps Generation Z (the generation leading the self-employment trend) in the future—are buying houses and apartments where domesticity incorporates work, business, and connectivity. The faddish work-live abodes of the 2000s provide a starting point for proposing living patterns for today's culture.

Ardmore House is located on a typical Chicago block at the intersection of an alleyway and a streetfront. By flipping the programmatic status quo of the typical domestic section, the design locates the kitchen, living, and dining spaces on the upper level, which has greater daylighting and grander ceiling height, and the bedrooms on the lower level, which receives less light. The reconfigured section matches both the tangible needs of light quality for each room and the intangible priorities favoring community to make for a new way of living.

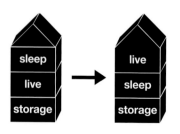

left: Flipped domestic section

opposite, top:
Second-floor ribbon window hovering above alleyway

opposite, bottom:
Study model along alley

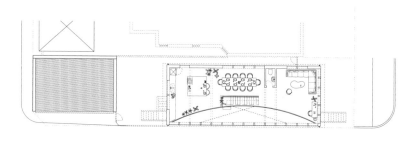

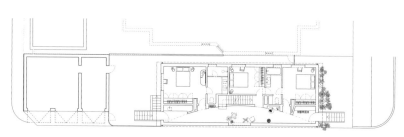

opposite, top:
Second floor

opposite, bottom:
Plans, levels 2 and 1

below: First-floor
interior courtyard open
to second floor

Grand Lattices
Chicago Prize Winning Proposal, Chicago Architectural Club
Chicago, Illinois, 2016

Grand Lattices, a proposal for a series of viewing decks along Lake Shore Drive, seeks to enhance the pedestrian's experience of Chicago and Lake Michigan. Lake Shore Drive—one of the most scenic highways in the United States—blocks street-level views from the city to the lake and vice versa. With entries at the median of each underpass along the drive, pedestrians can walk up the stairs of *Grand Lattices* to take in new vantage points that bridge Lake Michigan and downtown Chicago.

Chicago is known for its steel-frame construction, which provides the bones for many of the city's notable buildings. *Grand Lattices* uses the same construction method, but without the cladding. Each viewing deck is a unique and singular form; an expansion of the vocabulary of the steel frame; a landmark connected to an underpass that leads to the waterfront and signals that it is just beyond.

The underpass—an often overlooked urban space—provides a new public space at the intersection of city and lake, park and highway. Lake Shore Drive is no longer a driving-only experience. For the new pedestrian users, it is a gateway to access the waterfront, see the city, and admire the lake.

opposite: Photocollages of *Grand Lattices* along North and South Lake Shore Drive

top: Underpass as a space to access *Grand Lattice* viewing deck above rather than a "through space"

bottom: Section

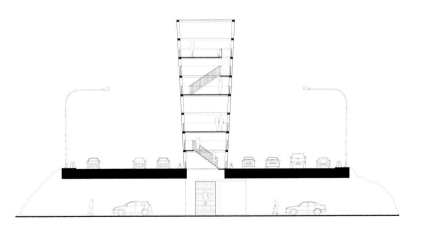

Table Top Apartments
New York Affordable Housing Challenge Winning Proposal
New York, New York, 2017

Table Top Apartments uses a system of modules based on stacking tabletops to generate multifamily residences at various scales: walk-up apartments, towers with setbacks and cascading balconies, even superblocks. The tabletop system is flexible enough for a range of lot sizes but also adaptable enough for a range of unit combinations. *Table Top Apartments* generates a new type of housing that is dense, diverse, open, and light-filled for residents to enjoy together.

The modular elements take the form of three unitary shapes (circle, square, rectangle). The apartment types made possible by the system suggest that diversity paired with density makes for a healthy and sustainable living environment. When the units are aggregated, they create both private balconies and shared public circulation; setting the modules in deliberately misaligned stacks produces vertical courtyards. The introduction of shared public spaces transforms the relationship between inhabitants and neighbors. A simple storefront glazing system divides interior from exterior; wood cabinets enclose private spaces and bathrooms.

opposite: View toward shared vertical courtyards

below and opposite:
Table Top superblock

top, left: Four-story walk-up on 25-by-100-foot lot

bottom: View from the cascading balconies

top, right: *Table Top* tower, Brooklyn

top: Slab
structural model

bottom, left:
Plan showing 3 two-
bedroom units,
1 one-bedroom unit,
and 2 studio units

bottom, right:
Circular, square,
and rectangular
table tops

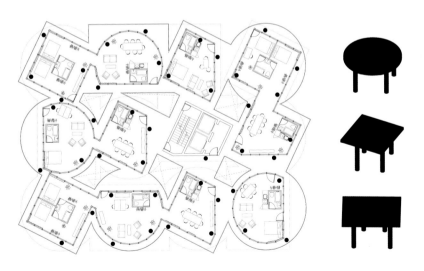

Towers within a Tower
Hong Kong Pixel Homes Competition Winning Proposal
Hong Kong, 2017

Individual apartment units are typically configured horizontally. In *Towers within a Tower*, they are organized vertically, with living areas stacked one atop the other. Each apartment therefore becomes its own tower, reproducing Hong Kong's urban verticality at the scale of a single residence.

Three basic apartment types—studios, one-bedrooms, and family units—ensure economical construction. Each type has a specific proportion, allocation of uses, and color. When the apartments are grouped, they produce shared outdoor spaces: a local neighborhood at every level.

The structure is prefabricated concrete; the "rooms" are stacked using cast-in steel-plate embeds. Colorful ceramic tiles cladding the concrete frame echo the material used for most residential towers in Hong Kong. The modular system can be used at different scales, from a four-story rural housing complex to a tower in the city, and with different mixes of apartments. As a system, the tower unit proposes a new residential typology: vertical living.

opposite, top: *Tower within a Tower* set within Hong Kong's urban field

opposite, bottom (left to right): Tower units: studio unit, one-bedroom unit, family unit

top: *Tower within a Tower* along street

bottom, left: The four rooms of a typical apartment unit (living room, kitchen, bedroom, and bathroom) transformed into

vertically stacked rooms; horizontal apartment units transformed into vertical apartment units

bottom, right: Plan of eight-unit *Tower within a Tower*

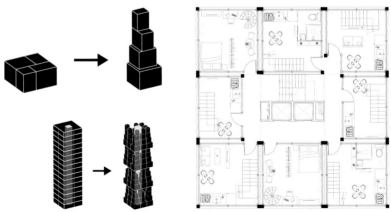

below: Open
access with a central,
light-filled core